Jesus' 30 recorded healings are retold in the following books:

Jesus' Healings, Part 1

Man Healed of Mental Illness (Capernaum)
Peter's Mother-in-Law Healed of Fever
Man Healed of Leprosy
Man Healed of Paralysis
Man with Withered Hand Healed
Nobleman's Son Healed of Illness
Centurion's Servant Healed of Paralysis
Widow's Son Brought Back to Life
Woman Healed of Sin
Man Healed of Blindness and Dumbness

Jesus' Healings, Part 2

Man Healed of Mental Illness (Gadara)
Jairus' Daughter Brought Back to Life
Woman Healed of Illness
Two Men Healed of Blindness
Man Healed of Dumbness
Man Healed of Disability
Woman's Daughter Healed of Illness
Man Healed of Deafness and Speech Problems
Man Healed of Blindness
Man's Son Healed of Epilepsy

Jesus' Healings, Part 3

Woman Healed of Back Problem
Man Healed of Swelling
Ten Men Healed of Leprosy
Woman Healed of Adultery
Man Healed of Blindness from Birth
Lazarus Brought Back to Life
Bartimaeus Healed of Blindness
Zacchaeus Healed of Dishonesty
Malchus' Ear Healed
Jesus' Resurrection

Other products by the authors and illustrator include the following:

- Ten Commandments Cards
- Beatitudes Cards
- Interactive Bible Time-Line

Jesus' healings
Part 2

Written by

Mary Jo Beebe
Olene E. Carroll
Nancy H. Fischer

Illustrated by

Genevieve Meek

Table of Contents

GENERAL PUBLICATIONS
BIBLE PRODUCTS, CSPS
Boston, Massachusetts, U.S.A.

ISBN: 87510-403-7
© 2002 General Publications Bible Products, CSPS
Printed in the United States of America

Introduction

About the Book

Jesus' Healings, Part 2, is the second in a three-part series. The three books are written for all ages—children, teenagers, and adults—anyone who is interested in the great healing work of Jesus.

All 30 of Jesus' Healings Included

The three books bring to life in simple language the 30 recorded healings of Christ Jesus. These healings span a period of possibly three years in Jesus' life. They include healings of sickness and sin, as well as four accounts of restoring life, one of them being Jesus' own resurrection.

Stories Arranged in Chronological Order

We have attempted to place the healings in chronological order according to Bible scholars. Not one of the Gospel writers includes all 30 of the healings. Some of the stories are found in only one Gospel book. In some cases, stories can be found in two of the books, sometimes in three, and two of them in all four. As a result, no exact chronology is known.

Account Chosen Based on Detail

When more than one account of a healing story occurs, in most cases we have chosen the account that is the richest in detail. When there are significant details in another account, we have added that information in sidebars.

Stories—Self-Contained

Each of the healing stories in the book is self-contained, with references to other pages in the book for definitions and commentary. While this feature is helpful for reading and studying individual stories, we recommend that you take the time to read the book from beginning to end as well. This will give you a full and inspired understanding of the scope and importance of Jesus' healings.

Written in Simple Language

The stories are written in contemporary English and at a level young children can understand. Sidebars provide additional information and commentary about the stories that will be interesting to older children and adults. In a few of the stories, passages too difficult for young children to understand have been placed in sidebars.

While every attempt has been made to write the stories in simple language, some stories may still be beyond the understanding of very young children. Parents and teachers must use their own discretion about the appropriateness of stories. In some cases, it may be helpful to paraphrase a story or leave out certain sections.

Details and Ideas Added for Understanding

In writing the stories, we have added details and ideas with the intent of making the stories more understandable. The details are supported by authoritative Bible scholars. You can find sources in the bibliography on page 59.

Based on Concepts in the Bible and *Science and Health with Key to the Scriptures*

In the healing stories, we have identified spiritual truths that were the foundation of Jesus' healings. These truths are based on concepts found in the Bible and in *Science and Health with Key to the Scriptures* by Mary Baker Eddy. *Science and Health* provides inspiring insights into the Scriptures, helping the reader recognize the spiritual ideas that were so important in Jesus' healings. These include Jesus' spiritual understanding of God, which enabled him to see beyond the material senses and to affirm the spiritual reality.

Introduction

Special Features of the Book

Jesus' Healings includes features you may want to explore before you read the stories. Understanding how the book is organized and arranged will enhance your enjoyment of it.

Sidebars like this provide information about a bolded word or phrase in the story.

Sidebars like this show where information can be found in another story about a bolded word or phrase in the story.

Sidebars like this provide commentary or information from another Gospel account. The sidebar color matches a colored square in the story for easy reference.

NOTE: All Bible quotations in sidebars are from the King James Version.

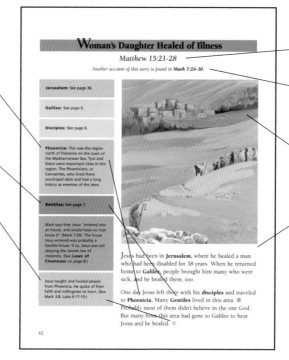

Bible book and verses where the story can be found.

Bible books and verses where other accounts of the story can be found.

Illustrations enhance children's (and adults') understanding and enjoyment of the stories.

The text is easily read and understood by all ages.

The end of each story is indicated by a large colored square.

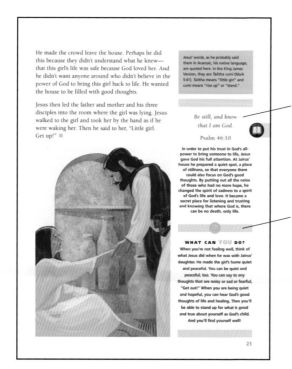

Bible verse sidebars provide a Bible verse with spiritual truths that Jesus would have known—also comments about the practicality of these truths to heal today.

The "What Can YOU Do?" sidebars provide ideas for children and teens that help them see how they can apply the spiritual truths in the healing story to their lives.

Introduction

Jesus and His Healing Mission

Christ Jesus' healings inspired the people of Palestine in the first century A.D., and they inspire us today. While Jesus' background was humble, his words and works were mighty.

Jesus grew to manhood knowing that his mission was God-directed. Luke reports that at the age of 30, Jesus began his ministry. It was in the synagogue in Nazareth, where he had grown up, that he announced to those who had known him as a child and now as a man, that he had a mission—one that the prophet Isaiah had told them about many years before. He stood to read it,

> The Spirit of the Lord is upon me, because he hath anointed me to preach the gospel to the poor; he hath sent me to heal the brokenhearted, to preach deliverance to the captives, and recovering of sight to the blind, to set at liberty them that are bruised, to preach the acceptable year of the Lord (Luke 4:18, 19).

All eyes were on this gentle, loving man as he told the people that this Scripture was fulfilled that day. They were in the presence of the man who was bringing good news to the world. This message of God's infinite power and love for His children would heal sickness and sin and restore life.

For the next three years, Jesus took this message into the cities and regions of Palestine. Matthew tells us: "And there followed him great multitudes of people from Galilee, and from Decapolis, and from Jerusalem, and from Judæa, and from beyond Jordan" (Matthew 4:25). Although most of Jesus' works occurred in Galilee, he also healed in other regions, such as Samaria and Phoenicia in Syria. "Beyond Jordan" refers to the regions to the east of the Jordan River that included Decapolis, Perea, and Gaulanitis.

He taught, he preached, he healed the sick and sinning, and he brought people back to life. The Bible records 30 individual healings. But it also tells us that Jesus healed many others. Here, Matthew tells of Jesus healing large numbers of people,

> And great multitudes came unto him, having with them those that were lame, blind, dumb, maimed, and many others, and cast them down at Jesus' feet; and he healed them: insomuch that the multitude wondered, when they saw the dumb to speak, the maimed to be whole, the lame to walk, and the blind to see: and they glorified the God of Israel (Matthew 15:30, 31).

Jesus sent out his closest disciples (as well as 70 others) to heal as he did. He told them,

> And as ye go, preach, saying, The kingdom of heaven is at hand. Heal the sick, cleanse the lepers, raise the dead, cast out devils: freely ye have received, freely give (Matthew 10:8).

And Jesus didn't leave his instruction to heal only with his disciples. It's clear that he expected all of his followers down through the ages to heal through spiritual means. He said,

> Verily, verily, I say unto you, He that believeth on me, the works that I do shall he do also; and greater works than these shall he do (John 14:12).

Introduction

Jesus' Times and the Dawn of the Messiah

Jesus was a Jew. His background was grounded in the Jewish belief in one God. He lived in a time when the Jews had very little control over their own lives. Many years before Jesus' time, Palestine was conquered by the Greeks. During that period, the Greeks tried to destroy the Jewish religion. Life for the Jews was extremely harsh. In 63 B.C. the Romans took over Palestine, and the Jews felt the enormous weight of that rule.

The major religious leaders of their times, referred to in the Bible as the scribes and Pharisees, developed a system of worship that was centered on everyday human observance of religious laws. Some of these laws were written; others were spoken. The intent of these laws was to help the Jews keep their faith centered in their belief in God. The effect, however, was that the laws were so restrictive and the details so minute that too often people focused on the laws more than on the inspiration and power of God.

This was the political and religious environment in which Jesus began his healing ministry.

Hundreds of years before Jesus' time and during periods of occupation of their lands by other countries, the Jewish people began to develop the idea that a Messiah would come some day to free them from their enemies. Many thought of this Messiah as a king from the family of David (see **Messiah/Christ** on page 5). Many thought of him as a priest. Others spoke of a prophet who would come. Old Testament prophets told of a coming Messiah and what could be expected when he came. In fact, when Jesus read from the prophet Isaiah one Sabbath day in the Nazareth synagogue, the passage was one that the Jews would have recognized as referring to such a Messiah.

But Jesus' idea of a Messiah was a new one. He brought people fresh insights about his mission. He brought them an understanding of the Messiah as a spiritual idea that would heal. This spiritual idea was his and everyone's relationship to God as God's spiritual, perfect children. If one had complete faith in this view of man created in God's image and likeness—whole, healthy, and free—and understood the all-power of God, then they would feel and experience the kingdom of heaven, or harmony. Healing would be the outcome. And Jesus proved this with wonderful, powerful healings. Multitudes of people came to Jesus to be healed. Seeing and experiencing healing, they began to realize that he must be the Messiah they had longed for.

Each step of the way in his ministry, Jesus worked to help the religious leaders and the people understand the concept of the Messiah he was presenting. But Jesus encountered much opposition. He was a threat to the scribes' and Pharisees' system of religion. As they saw it, they were in danger of losing their Jewish following if the people accepted Jesus' teachings.

The scribes and Pharisees were focused on their materialistic system of worship and their need to preserve this system. They refused to recognize Jesus' works as evidence of the Spirit or power of God—the basis of his system of healing. This prevented most of them from seeing the spiritual import of Jesus' teachings and healings. This was an import that blessed the world then and continues to bless as spiritual healing finds its rightful place in the 21st century.

Introduction

The Messiah/Christ concept is central to an understanding of Jesus and his healings. Many of the healing stories that follow will refer to this information about the Messiah/Christ.

Messiah/Christ: The Hebrew word for "Messiah" and the Greek word for "Christ" mean "anointed"—chosen and dedicated—to save or deliver. Many Jews believed the Messiah of the Old Testament was a special anointed king from the family of David, who would come someday. This king, the "Son of David," would get rid of all their enemies and set up a kingdom that would last forever. Other Jews believed the Messiah would be a priest who would purify the way Israel worshiped God. And others saw that a prophet like Moses would come. Isaiah told of a Messiah who would be a light not just for Jews but for the whole world. To the Jews, light was a symbol of God's purity and goodness, which would save people from all their troubles.

Before Jesus' birth, Mary was told by an angel that her son would be great and would be called the Son of the Highest and that God would give him the throne of David. It was said at Jesus' birth that a Saviour, Christ the Lord, was born. John the Baptist prophesied that a Messiah was to come, one who was "mightier" than he.

At the beginning of Jesus' ministry, when he read from Isaiah in the Nazareth synagogue, he declared that he was "anointed" by the Spirit to be the great prophet described in Isaiah, one who would bless all by helping the poor and captives and healing people. Later, when John the Baptist sent his disciples to Jesus to ask him if he was the Messiah, Jesus referred them to his "works"—"the blind see, the lame walk, the lepers are cleansed, the deaf hear, the dead are raised, to the poor the gospel is preached" (Luke 7:22).

Jesus didn't think of himself as an earthly king. He saw his role as fulfilling the scripture to heal and teach and to bring to light the "kingdom of God"—the reign of harmony. He saw the Christ as his—and everyone's—spiritual selfhood. He knew that God created man in His image and likeness and kept him that way. Therefore, man is always spiritual, whole, and complete. Jesus never allowed the material picture of sickness, sin, and death to have power or reality in his thought.

By knowing that the Christ, or his spiritual selfhood, was the only truth or reality, Jesus destroyed the "enemies" of sickness, sin, and death. And this understanding of the Christ brought the "kingdom of God"—complete harmony.

Jesus' life, teachings, and spiritual healings showed how clearly he understood his spiritual selfhood. People began to give him the title of "Christ," calling him "Christ Jesus." Christ Jesus is an example for us all. We, too, can heal as he commanded his followers to do, by understanding God's all-power and our spiritual relationship to Him.

In the recorded stories of Jesus' healings, names that refer to the Messiah are:

Christ
Holy One of God
Prophet
Son of David
Son of the Most High God
Light of the World
Son of God

Man Healed of Mental Illness (Gadara)

Luke 8:26-39

*Other accounts of this story are found in **Matthew 8:28-34** and **Mark 5:1-20**.*

Galilee: This was the region in the north of Palestine in which Jesus grew up and spent most of his healing ministry. Almost all the disciples came from Galilee.

Disciples: The Greek word for "disciple" means "learner," or "student." In the New Testament, this word often refers to Jesus' 12 disciples. But it could mean anyone—man, woman, or child—who is a student and follower of the ideas of a teacher.

See Matthew 8:23-27; Mark 4:35-41; Luke 8:22-25.

Jesus had been teaching and healing people in **Galilee,** in the towns and countryside near the beautiful lake called the Sea of Galilee.

One day Jesus got into a boat with his **disciples.** He said to them, "Let's go to the other side of the lake." So they started off.

During the trip a huge storm came up. The wind was very strong, and the waves were so high that the disciples were afraid the boat would turn over. But Jesus wasn't afraid. He ordered the wind and waves to be still. And they were!

Then, Jesus and his disciples were able to continue their trip across the lake. ▪

Soon, they arrived in the land of the Gadarenes  in **Decapolis,** where many **Gentiles** lived. Gentiles were people who didn't believe in the one God, and the Jews didn't want to be near them. Perhaps the disciples were not eager to go to this land. But Jesus loved everyone and was always ready to help and heal.

When they got to the shore, a man ▨ came toward Jesus shouting. This man had been mentally ill for a long time. He was as wild and as loud as the thundering storm on the lake had been. And he didn't wear the kind of clothes other people wore.

The exact location of this story is not known. Matthew says that the people were called "Gergesenes," meaning that they came from the town of Gergesa on the Sea of Galilee (Matthew 8:28). Mark and Luke tell us that the people were called "Gadarenes," meaning that they came from Gadara or an area around Gadara. Gadara is in the region of Decapolis (Mark 5:1; Luke 8:26). (See **Decapolis** below.)

Decapolis: This was the region east of Samaria and Galilee. It was originally called "Decapolis" because ten cities in the area formed an association for trade and security reasons. The word "Decapolis" is formed from two Greek words: *deca,* meaning "ten," and *polis,* meaning "city."

Gentiles: People who did not believe in the one God were called "Gentiles" by the Jews. Because Gentiles worshiped other gods, Jews considered them "unclean," or impure. So the Jews separated themselves from Gentiles to keep their religion pure. (See **Laws of Cleanness** on page 8.)

Matthew says there were two wild men, who were "exceeding fierce, so that no man might pass by that way" (Matt 8:28).

Caves: Caves were sometimes used as tombs or burial places. People believed that devils lived in dark places like caves.

Mark adds that the man was so unhappy he screamed and cut himself with sharp stones (Mark 5:5).

Unclean Spirits, Evil Spirits, Demons, Devils, Unclean Devils: In Jesus' time people believed there were invisible beings that could get inside them, could speak for them, and could cause many kinds of diseases and disabilities. They believed these beings worked for the Devil or Satan (words that refer to that which is opposed to God). In the Bible, "unclean" means "impure." (See **Laws of Cleanness** below.)

Laws of Cleanness: These were laws the Jews believed they needed to obey in order to be "clean" or pure in the sight of God. They believed that the sick, the sinning, the dead, Gentiles (see **Gentiles** on page 7), certain animals such as swine and dogs, and people controlled by what they called unclean spirits were "unclean" or impure. They believed that if they touched or were touched by someone or something that was unclean, they became unclean, too. To be clean or pure again, the unclean had to take part in special purification rituals.

The man didn't live in a house but, instead, stayed in dark **caves.** Sometimes he was so out of control that people tied his hands and feet with chains to try to calm him down. But he was so strong that he broke the chains and ran wild into the desert.

In those days people were superstitious and believed in **devils,** or **unclean spirits.** They believed these devils, or spirits, were invisible beings that could make them sick and mentally ill. They thought devils were making this man wild and out of control. But Jesus didn't believe that. He knew that what people called devils were not real beings. They were just bad or wild thoughts that had no power.

What would Jesus do when he met this man?

8

The first thing Jesus did was to give a strong order, "**Come out of the man, you unclean spirit!**"

As Jesus looked at this man, he saw what others didn't see. He saw the man God created—calm, clear thinking, orderly, in control. Jesus knew there is only one Spirit, which is God—and this calm and peaceful Spirit is everywhere. There is no room for any other spirit. God doesn't create unclean spirits, or wild thoughts and actions. All He creates is good.

Casting Out Devils: Often Matthew, Mark, and Luke describe Jesus as "casting out devils" (see **Unclean Spirits, Evil Spirits, Demons, Devils, Unclean Devils** on page 8). Jesus also told his followers to cast out devils. In Bible times most people believed superstitions about devils and demons. They thought that diseases, disasters, and unhappiness were caused by devils, invisible beings who were everywhere—in the water, the air, the desert, the fields, the night, and even inside people. Magicians invented elaborate rituals to get rid of the devils. Superstitious people believed these rituals made the devils leave. But they also believed the devils could move back in.

Jesus never believed devils were real. In fact, he was always helping people wake up from superstitious beliefs to see that the only power anywhere is God's power of good. And he didn't use rituals to cast out devils, which he knew were only bad thoughts. The Bible tells us he cast out devils by the "Spirit of God" and by his "word" (Matthew 12:28; Matthew 8:16). The Bible also tells us that Jesus "commanded" devils to come out. Jesus knew that God gave him the ability and authority to get rid of any thought that was not good. He knew devils, or bad thoughts, did not have any place, power, or reality. People felt the influence of Jesus' prayer that God is the only power. It helped remove their fears. When the fears were gone, so were the diseases and sins.

The Bible calls this "casting out devils." Today we might call it "casting out evil"—getting rid of any bad thoughts by understanding that only good is real and present.

Messiah/Christ: See page 5.

See Matthew 4:23-25.

WHAT CAN YOU DO?

Some kids you know might believe in different kinds of superstitions. They might talk to you about evil spirits, devils, ghosts, or haunted houses. Or they might talk to you about luck—either good or bad luck. For example, some might believe it's good luck to pick a certain number or wear a special charm. Others might believe it's bad luck to see a black cat or to walk under a ladder.

These kids may just be joking or trying to scare you, or they may really believe that these superstitions are true. Jesus knew that evil spirits and superstitions are not real and have no power. God is the only Spirit and is all good. And because God's power of good governs you every minute, superstition of any kind is no part of your life. When you know this, nothing can scare you, because you are right in the center of God's love. And you can help other kids know this, too!

When Jesus told the unclean spirit to leave, the man fell down at Jesus' feet. He shouted, "What do you want with me, Jesus, Son of the Most High God? I beg you—don't bother me." "Son of the Most High God" was another name for "**Messiah**" or "**Christ.**" These were names the Jews used for a special king or prophet they believed would come one day to help and heal them. Some Gentiles in Decapolis had traveled to Galilee and had heard of this Jewish Messiah. Perhaps some had seen or heard of Jesus and his healings. ▓ Some probably heard that he might even be the Messiah.

This man knew Jesus had the power to cast out devils. But at that moment, perhaps the man didn't think that devils, or wild thoughts, were controlling him. He believed it was normal for him to be wild. Therefore, he wanted to be left alone.

But Jesus cared about the man. He wouldn't leave him, and he wouldn't give up. Jesus wasn't fooled by the wild thoughts because he knew they were just lies. He knew that only God was in control of this man's thinking, and he wanted to help the man see this, too.

Jesus was always praying, always listening for what God was telling him to do. So he faced this man calmly and asked him, "What is your name?" People's names had special meaning in those days. Their names told what they were like or what their nature was. So Jesus was asking the man to think about what he was believing about himself.

The man gave Jesus an answer that may have seemed strange. Instead of telling Jesus his real name, he told him his name was "Legion." The man didn't know why he gave this answer. Legion wasn't his name. It was a word meaning a group of about 6,000 soldiers.

Perhaps Jesus' question helped the man see that he had let many devils, or wild thoughts, get him so mixed up that he had forgotten who he really was. This question helped him remember. At that point, he probably realized those devils were not part of him, and he wanted them out of his life.

And right in front of him was Jesus—just the one who could help him.

In this story, devils, or unclean spirits, are described as speaking. But this is impossible because devils, or unclean spirits, are not real. So when Matthew, Mark, and Luke say that devils talked to Jesus, it means that the mentally ill man spoke aloud what he was believing was true. The man believed that devils controlled him and spoke through him.

The Deep: People believed "the deep," or "the abyss," was a bottomless pit where devils, or unclean spirits, were sent for their final punishment. Some believed the deep was the place of the dead, or hell. People were very afraid of the deep.

Mark tells us that the man didn't want the devils to go "out of the country," which means areas where no one lived. The people were superstitious and believed that these areas were haunted by devils and spirits (Mark 5:10).

Mark says the herd consisted of 2,000 swine (pigs) (Mark 5:13). Before pigs were tamed and before they were cared for by herders, they ran wild and were called boars. We don't know what the pigs in this story looked like, but a wild boar could weigh about 400 pounds. It had long bristles, five-inch tusks that were very sharp, and a long nose used for digging up roots to eat. It could be frightened easily and could run very fast.

Jesus knew the man now wanted to be healed. But the man still thought devils were real, and he was afraid of them. He believed the devils had to obey Jesus and leave, but he also believed he had to keep them happy so they wouldn't hurt him.

The man believed there might be a couple of ways to get rid of the devils. ■ One way was for them to go to a place called "**the deep.**" ■ The other way was for them to go into someone or something else.

The first way—to go into the deep—probably didn't seem like a good choice to the man. Like many other people at that time, he believed the deep was a place where the devils would be punished. And he believed they wouldn't like to go there and might hurt him if they were sent there.

So the man thought the other way of getting rid of the devils would be better. This was for them to go into a herd of pigs ■ he saw on the hill nearby. The man believed the devils would be happy to go into the pigs and wouldn't hurt him when they did.

Jesus knew the man wasn't completely ready to let go of his beliefs about devils. Jesus didn't try to make him understand everything at once. He knew that sometimes people have to take one step at a time in order to give up old beliefs and to understand God and His great power. So he let the man believe the devils went into the pigs.

When the pigs were suddenly frightened by something and ran down the steep hillside into the lake, the man believed the devils were destroyed. The man was very superstitious—just like his neighbors. He seemed to need to see this in order to know he was free of the devils.

But Jesus had always known that devils were not real. Therefore, he knew they didn't have any power to move from one place to another. He knew that God, Spirit, is the only power and is everywhere. Devils, or wild thoughts, have no power or place to be.

From the first time Jesus met this man, he saw only a perfect man, made in the pure, spiritual likeness of God, who is Spirit. By seeing this man as God's likeness, Jesus healed him.

*Resist the devil, and
he will flee from you.*

James 4:7

Jesus always listened to and obeyed God, who is the only power. When other people were fooled into believing there were other powers, called devils, or unclean spirits, Jesus was able to help them. He knew that so-called devils were only bad or wild thoughts. He showed people that they didn't have to give in to bad thoughts. He knew that God gives everyone the strength to resist, or to stand up to, bad thoughts.

When Jesus told the devil, or unclean spirit, to come out of the man, he was showing his understanding of God's power. This understanding was like a bright light chasing the darkness away. God gives us all the strength we need to stand bravely and say "No" to bad thoughts. Then, they disappear for us, too.

As soon as the man knew the devils were gone, he was free of fear. He was ready for the next step. He was ready to learn about God's all-power and about himself as the child of God.

The pig herders, who saw what happened, ran to tell other people. Many from the countryside and the town hurried to see for themselves. ■

And what a wonderful sight they saw! The wild man they had all been so afraid of wasn't wild any more. He was sitting quietly and peacefully at Jesus' feet. He must have been listening to Jesus teach, just like a disciple would. He was dressed and in his right mind—thinking calm, good thoughts.

The man was completely healed.

14

When the superstitious people saw that this man was healed, they were afraid because they didn't understand how this healing happened. They asked Jesus to go back across the lake to his own home. So Jesus and the disciples began to get into their boat.

The man who was healed was so thankful for his healing that he begged to go with Jesus. But Jesus had something much more important for this man to do.

"Go back to your home," Jesus told the man. "You must tell the people there what great things God has done for you." ▮

And that's exactly what the man did! Not only did he tell his friends and family, but he also went throughout his city telling everyone how wonderful it was that Jesus had healed him. ▮ How happy he must have been!

Mark adds that the man began to tell people throughout Decapolis about his wonderful healing and about Jesus. According to Mark, when the people heard the man tell his story, they marvelled, which means they were in awe or amazed (Mark 5:20).

Perhaps this man of Gadara was the first apostle to the Gentiles. (An apostle is a person who is sent out to take a message to others.)

When Jesus visited this land again, he found that many Gentiles followed him—listening to him and asking for healing. (See "Man Healed of Deafness and Speech Problems," page 47.) Jesus even fed over 4,000 Gentiles in this land with seven loaves of bread and a few fishes (Matthew 15:29-38; Mark 8:1-9). The Gadarene must have been a good apostle to spread the word!

Jairus' Daughter Brought Back to Life

Mark 5:21-24, 35-43

*Other accounts of this story are found in **Matthew 9:18, 19, 23-26** and **Luke 8:40-42, 49-56**.*

Disciples: See page 6.

Capernaum: This was a small city in Galilee where Jesus began his ministry. People with products of all kinds traveled through the city to the Mediterranean and Damascus. Roman soldiers were stationed there. Many people in Capernaum, including some of Jesus' disciples, earned their living as fishermen on the Sea of Galilee.

Matthew tells us Jesus "came into his own city" (Matthew 9:1). Jesus made Capernaum his home during his ministry and healed many people there.

Sabbath/Synagogue: The Jews met in the synagogue to worship God on the Sabbath day, which is Saturday. Inside the synagogue were benches along the walls, a raised platform, oil lamps, and a cabinet to hold the Scriptures on scrolls. Men and women may have sat in separate places. "Chief seats" were reserved for elders and important visitors. Jesus once rebuked the **scribes and Pharisees** (see page 32) for taking these seats so that people could see them. The service consisted of prayer, singing psalms, reading from the Scriptures, and teaching. The man in charge, the "ruler," chose men to read and teach. Jesus was chosen to teach in synagogues many times.

After Jesus healed a man in Gadara of mental illness, he and his **disciples** crossed the Sea of Galilee to return to **Capernaum.**

When they got to the shore, a big crowd was waiting for Jesus. They were all so happy he was back in town. One of the people in the crowd was a man named Jairus. He was the ruler of the **synagogue,** the place where the Jews met to learn about God. Jairus' job as ruler, or leader, was to take care of the synagogue and to be in charge of the meetings held there. He had come to Jesus because he needed help.

Jairus fell down at Jesus' feet and begged him, saying, "My little daughter is dying.  Please come and **heal her.**  I want her to live!"

Matthew says that Jairus told Jesus his daughter was already dead (Matthew 9:18).

Matthew and Mark tell us that Jairus asked Jesus to come and lay his hands on his daughter so that she would be healed (Matthew 9:18; Mark 5:23). (See **Laying on of Hands** below.)

Laying on of Hands/Healing by Touch: In Bible times many people believed they could be healed when they were touched by Jesus or when they touched him or his clothing.

☐ *Being touched by Jesus ("laying on of hands"):* The term, "laying on of hands," was a symbol for the power of God to heal. To Jesus, placing hands on someone didn't mean that the human hands had any real power in them to bless or to heal. Instead, it was an expression of love and compassion that helped remove the person's fear. In half of Jesus' 30 recorded healings, no mention of Jesus touching the person is made. In three of these cases, he healed people who were not even present with him. And in many of the healing stories, when Jesus touched people, the Bible records that he made it clear it was their faith that healed them.

☐ *Touching Jesus or his clothing:* Many people believed that if they touched Jesus or his clothing they would be healed. Jesus was so spiritually minded that he was able to know people's need for healing. Those who reached out were healed because of Jesus' clear understanding of the all-power of God, who is Spirit, to heal.

See the following stories in *Jesus' Healings, Part 1:*

☐ "Man Healed of Mental Illness (Capernaum)," page 6.

☐ "Peter's Mother-in-Law Healed of Fever," page 12.

☐ "Man Healed of Paralysis," page 20.

☐ "Man with Withered Hand Healed," page 29.

See "Woman Healed of Illness," page 25.

Jairus probably knew that Jesus was a great healer. In Capernaum, Jesus had healed people of mental illness, fever, and paralysis. In that area he had also healed a man with a withered hand and probably many others. ▪

On this day, as always, Jesus was ready and willing to heal. He agreed to go with Jairus.

Jairus may have been one of the happiest people in the crowd. Now, he had hope that his 12-year-old daughter would be healed.

As Jesus started walking with Jairus to his house, lots of people followed him and crowded around him. One of these people was a woman who had been sick for many years. ▪ Moving through the crowd and coming up behind Jesus, she reached out and touched his cloak. She knew she was healed when she did this.

Jesus stopped and turned to the woman to tell her that it was her faith that healed her. ▨ While he was talking, a messenger from Jairus' house came to Jairus with some very bad news. He said, "Your daughter is dead. Why bother the **teacher** any more?"

Both Jairus and the woman believed that touch was needed to bring healing. Jairus wanted Jesus to lay his hands on his daughter, and the woman thought she had been healed by touching Jesus' cloak. When Jesus told the woman that it was her faith that healed her, it may have helped both the woman and Jairus understand that healing doesn't come through touch but through faith in God's power.

Teacher/Master: The Hebrew and Greek words that mean "teacher" or "master" were titles of respect. People called Jesus by these titles not because he had gone to a special school. It was because he spoke with great power and understanding when he taught about God and His laws.

The minute Jesus heard this, he said to Jairus, "Don't be afraid. Just keep **believing.**" Jesus wanted Jairus to keep his faith that his daughter would be healed.

Jairus had just seen the woman healed and had heard Jesus tell her that it was her faith that healed her. This must have given Jairus hope and helped him see how important faith was in order for his daughter to be brought back to life.

Peter, James, and John:
Perhaps these three men were more spiritually minded than the other disciples, and Jesus could trust them to pray quietly even when they didn't understand everything Jesus did. Jesus chose these three disciples to be with him on several special occasions.

Jewish Mourning Customs:
In Bible times, when someone died, people visited the person's family to show their love and to help them. The usual mourning period for family members was seven days.

The Jews also followed certain rituals to show their grief. Those in mourning wore clothes made of sackcloth—a rough, dark-colored material made of goat's or camel's hair. Often they "rent," or tore, their clothes. Some put ashes or dust on their heads.

Immediately after a person died, the family hired "mourners" (usually women) to weep and wail—to cry out very loudly and sing sad songs. They also hired people to play musical instruments, most often flutes. The Jewish laws said that even the poorest burial must have at least two flutes and one wailing woman.

Jesus went on with Jairus to his house but let only three of his disciples—**Peter, James, and John**— follow them.

When they got to the house, people were there **crying very loudly.** Others were playing flutes that made very sad sounds. This was their way to let others in the neighborhood know that the girl had died and to show how sad they were about her death.

21

Laws of Cleanness—Death:
The Jews believed that the dead were "unclean," or impure. Jewish laws said that anyone who touched a dead body or bier (bed) on which a dead body lay was considered unclean, or impure. The laws also said that anyone who entered the house where a dead body was laid would be unclean. The unclean person was supposed to follow certain rituals to become clean, or pure, again. When Jesus entered Jairus' house and took Jairus' daughter by the hand, he was considered unclean. (See **Laws of Cleanness** below.)

Laws of Cleanness: See page 8.

Jesus **went into the house** and said something to the people that surprised them. He asked, "Why are you crying and making such a fuss? She's not dead. She's just asleep."

Since the people knew that the girl was dead, they couldn't understand what Jesus meant when he said she was sleeping. They laughed and made fun of him for saying something they must have thought was very strange.

But Jesus' words showed he knew death was not the end of life. The death that seemed so real was like sleep that the girl could wake up from. Jesus was always listening to God's thoughts—thoughts of life and love and joy. He knew that God was in control. He knew that God is Life and that God gives life, not death, to His children.

Next, Jesus did something else that must have surprised the people who were crying and making loud noises.

He made the crowd leave the house. Perhaps he did this because they didn't understand what he knew—that this girl's life was safe because God loved her. And he didn't want anyone around who didn't believe in the power of God to bring this girl back to life. He wanted the house to be filled with good thoughts.

Jesus then led the father and mother and his three disciples into the room where the girl was lying. Jesus walked to the girl and took her by the hand as if he were waking her. Then he said to her, "Little girl. Get up!" ■

Jesus' words, as he probably said them in Aramaic, his native language, are quoted here. In the King James Version, they are *Talitha cumi* (Mark 5:41). *Talitha* means "little girl" and *cumi* means "rise up" or "stand."

Be still, and know that I am God.

Psalm 46:10

In order to put his trust in God's all-power to bring someone to life, Jesus gave God his full attention. At Jairus' house he prepared a quiet spot, a place of stillness, so that everyone there could also focus on God's good thoughts. By putting out all the noise of those who had no more hope, he changed the spirit of sadness to a spirit of God's life and love. It became a secret place for listening and trusting and knowing that where God is, there can be no death, only life.

?

WHAT CAN YOU DO?
When you're not feeling well, think of what Jesus did when he was with Jairus' daughter. He made the girl's home quiet and peaceful. You can be quiet and peaceful, too. You can say to any thoughts that are noisy or sad or fearful, "Get out!" When you are being quiet and hopeful, you can hear God's good thoughts of life and healing. Then you'll be able to stand up for what is good and true about yourself as God's child. And you'll find yourself well!

Luke adds that "her spirit came again." The word "spirit" in Greek is *pneuma* and can also mean "breath" or "life." This means that the girl came to life and began to breathe (Luke 8:55).

"Don't tell anyone. . . .": Jesus told some of the people he healed not to tell anyone about their healings. Here are some possible reasons why he said this:

☐ The people he healed were inspired and grateful. If they spoke out, the scribes and Pharisees (see **Scribes, Pharisees,** page 32) might ask them questions they weren't ready for. Perhaps Jesus was protecting them. He didn't want them to lose their faith and inspiration.

☐ People might come to Jesus just to see something exciting happen. They might crowd out those who really wanted to learn about God.

☐ If crowds gathered around Jesus, the Jewish religious leaders might become jealous and try to get rid of him.

☐ Crowds might start calling Jesus "Messiah." Many of them were expecting an earthly king to save them. Jesus needed time to teach the people and show them by healing and raising the dead what the Messiah really was—the spiritual selfhood belonging to him and everyone. He wanted them to see that he expressed this Christ, and they could, too. (See **Messiah/Christ** on page 5.)

Matthew adds that the news about this spread throughout the area (Matthew 9:26).

And, instantly, the girl got up and walked! ▪

Everyone in the room was amazed. They probably wanted to rush out and tell everyone all about it.

But Jesus ordered them **not to tell anyone** what had happened. ▪ He wanted them to be thankful in a quiet way for God's love and great goodness that had brought them all so much happiness.

Next, since Jesus knew the girl might be hungry, he told them to get her something to eat. How thoughtful he was! Everyone there could see that the girl was just fine.

Imagine how happy the girl's mother and father were that their daughter was alive and completely well!

Woman Healed of Illness

Mark 5:25-34

*Other accounts of this story are found in **Matthew 9:20-22** and **Luke 8:43-48**.*

Disciples: See page 6.

Capernaum: See page 16.

The Bible says this woman had "an issue of blood" (Matthew 9:20; Mark 5:25; Luke 8:43). The Greek phrase means "flow of blood."

Laws of Cleanness: See page 8.

Jesus and his **disciples** were in **Capernaum** and were on their way to Jairus' house. Jairus had asked Jesus to heal his daughter.

One of the people nearby was a woman who had been sick ■ for 12 years. She had spent all her money on doctors who she hoped would make her well—but none of them could help. In fact, she felt even worse. She probably thought she would never be well again.

Besides being sick, the woman was treated very unkindly by other people. They didn't want her to touch them or even get near them. This was because a Jewish law said that anyone who had a sickness like this was "**unclean**," which means "impure." How lonely she must have felt.

Laying on of Hands/Healing by Touch: See page 17.

Matthew says the woman "touched the hem of his garment" (Matthew 9:20). Luke says she "touched the border of his garment" (Luke 8:44). The "hem" or "border" in Greek means "tassels" or "fringe." Often, in the Bible the word for "garment" refers to a "cloak." Jesus was probably wearing a cloak, which was a large piece of material made of wool. Many cloaks may have had tassels at each of the four corners. Each tassel was tied with a blue thread. The tassels reminded the Jews of God's law and their duty to obey this law (Numbers 15:37-41). People believed the tassels were very holy.

Mark says "her blood was dried up" (Mark 5:29). Luke says "her issue of blood stanched" (Luke 8:44). These two phrases mean that the bleeding stopped.

This woman heard about Jesus and how he healed people through God's power. She must have watched him as he walked with Jairus to his house. A huge crowd of people followed them. Many gathered around Jesus, eager to be close to him. Perhaps the woman noticed how peaceful he was. She thought to herself, "If only I can **touch** his clothes, I'll be well."

Even though she knew that people didn't want her to be near them, she bravely slipped into the crowd. Without a word she moved up behind Jesus, reached out, and touched the tassels or fringe on his cloak. ▉ The minute she did this, she was healed ▉ —and she knew it right away.

And Jesus knew it right away, too. Jesus knew that God created His children in His likeness. This means God's children are perfect, healthy, and whole—and God always keeps them that way. Jesus knew these thoughts had healed someone. ▪

Immediately, Jesus turned around and asked, "Who touched my clothes?"

Jesus' disciples said to him, "How can you ask who touched you? Lots of people are touching and pushing you."

But Jesus didn't answer the disciples. Instead, he kept looking around to see who had done this.

Both Mark and Luke say that Jesus knew "virtue" went out of him (Mark 5:30; Luke 8:46). This word can also be translated "power."

And God said, Let us make man in our image, after our likeness. . . . And God saw every thing that he made, and, behold, it was very good.

Genesis 1:26, 31

Jesus knew that God is Spirit. Therefore, everyone is the image and likeness (or reflection) of Spirit. Everyone is spiritual and is always good and perfect. Jesus was always praying—always keeping his thought close to God. Even in a crowd of strangers, Jesus knew each one was God's reflection, good and perfect. Good thoughts like this are powerful. They heal. What Jesus knew then is the truth about everyone now, and forever. We can know this truth and heal today, too.

Jesus' Treatment of Women:
In Bible times people believed that women were less important than men. Many people thought of a daughter as just another mouth to feed. But a son could work for the family and carry on the father's name. Women were the property of their fathers or husbands. Yet they couldn't choose their husbands. Women had few opportunities to work. Therefore, a single woman might not be able to care for herself. She needed a man to help her—a father, brother, or son. Women were considered "unclean" for things that are natural to women, such as having babies. Most women were not educated. They couldn't read or teach in a synagogue. They weren't permitted to speak out in public. A man wasn't supposed to talk in public to a woman who was not related to him.

But Jesus was a reformer and introduced a new view of women. He treated them as equal to men. He spoke to them in the streets and synagogues. He taught women. He healed women. He included them in his parables. Women traveled with him and became his disciples. Two of his closest friends were Mary and Martha. Jesus helped women discover their individuality, freedom, and equality.

Matthew and Luke add that Jesus told the woman, "Be of good comfort" (Matthew 9:22; Luke 8:48). The word "comfort" in Greek means "to have courage" or "to be of good cheer."

The woman must have been amazed at her quick healing—as well as very thankful for it. When Jesus asked who touched him, she was afraid to speak up in front of everyone. Women never did that. She was also afraid to say she was the one who touched Jesus, since she had broken a Jewish law. This law said that an unclean person should not touch other people because it would make them unclean, too. And she didn't know what Jesus and the others would do if they found out.

But she had just been healed by Jesus. She must have felt that this loving man would be kind to her. This feeling was stronger than her fears. So she came forward and fell down at Jesus' feet. She told him that she had touched his cloak, and why, and that she was healed right away.

Jesus spoke to her kindly and lovingly, calling her the sweet name of "daughter." ■ His great kindness healed her fears.

Healing by Faith: See page 20.

Peace: The word "peace" is used throughout the Bible. The Hebrew word for peace, *shalom*, has a rich variety of meanings including prosperity, well-being, wholeness, health, security, harmony, happiness, quietness, calmness, rest, at one again.

WHAT CAN YOU DO?

If others are unkind to you, you might feel sad and lonely like this woman did. You can know that God is your Father-Mother and is your best friend. God is always loving you. Ask God, with all your heart, to help you feel that love. Listen for the good thoughts He gives you. Look for good wherever you are. Each time you hear or see something good, even if it seems very small, this shows that God's goodness and love are right where you are. You'll soon find that God's love is always bigger than any sadness or loneliness or unkindness. You'll find friendship and happiness everywhere.

Then Jesus said to the woman, "Your faith has made you well." He wanted her to know that the tassels she touched had no healing power. It was her **faith** that healed her.

Her faith was strong. She never gave up hope. She trusted that if Jesus used God's power to heal others, he could heal her, also. She expected to be healed. This faith was the important thing.

Then Jesus said a wonderful "good-bye" to the woman that would help her know God would always take care of her. He said, "Go in **peace.** Be free and be well!"

Two Men Healed of Blindness

Matthew 9:27-31

Capernaum: See page 16.

Messiah/Christ: See page 5.

Healing by Faith: See page 20.

Sir/Lord: These terms are titles of respect and refer to a person of authority.

WHAT CAN YOU DO?

Do you know people who are always saying that things won't work out right? That way of thinking makes it hard for them to hear God's healing messages. Because God is good and the only power, you can expect things to work out just right. That's what faith is—believing and expecting good. Faith lets us hear God's messages loud and clear. Faith brings healing. You can help others have faith in the power of good, too!

Jesus was in **Capernaum** where he brought a young girl back to life. When he left the girl's house, two blind men followed him, begging him for help. They called out, "Have mercy on us, Son of David!" They were hoping Jesus would be kind and heal them. The name they called Jesus—"Son of David"—meant "**Messiah,**" or "**Christ.**" These men, like many Jews, believed the Messiah was a special king that God would send to help and heal them.

Jesus went into a house, and the blind men followed him. Inside, without the large crowd around him, Jesus could talk quietly to the men. He turned to them and said, "Do you believe that I can heal you?" He wanted to help them see that it was important to have **faith**— to expect healing. They were very sure about their answer. They said, "Yes, **Lord!**"

Jesus then **touched** their eyes. Since they couldn't see him, this was such a loving thing to do. It helped them feel that Jesus cared about them. Jesus didn't believe that blindness was the truth about these men. He knew that God, who is Spirit, sees each of His children as spiritual and perfect. And all of God's children can see as perfectly as their Father.

As he touched them, Jesus said, "You believed you could be healed, and you *are* healed!" And they were! Can you imagine how very happy they were to be able to see?

What Jesus said next may have seemed a little strange to them.

Laying on of Hands/Healing by Touch: See page 17.

I am come a light into the world, that whosoever believeth on me should not abide in darkness.

John 12:46

Jesus had complete faith in the truth that everyone is made in God's image and, therefore, is always spiritual, good, and perfect. This truth of our spiritual selfhood is like light. When light is present, darkness is seen for what it is—nothing. When the truth of our spiritual selfhood fills our thought, the darkness of sickness, sin, and death disappears, and we are healed. Jesus proved this when he healed the two blind men instantly. Today, we have this same light of truth to help us. No matter how dark the trouble may seem, we can shine the light of truth on it, and see that trouble disappear.

"Don't tell anyone....": See page 24.

Scribes: These were men who copied the Jewish law (the "Torah"—the first five books of the Bible—which includes the Commandments) onto scrolls from other scrolls. They studied the Torah as well as many unwritten laws. Some scribes taught the meaning of all these laws and how people should obey them. But the scribes simply quoted words. Their teaching lacked the authority of Jesus' teaching. Jesus taught with absolute, unquestioned confidence in God's all-power. And this teaching resulted in healing.

Pharisees: The Pharisees were a group of men who loved to obey the Ten Commandments. But they also obeyed hundreds of other laws made by Jews through the years. Many Jews looked up to the Pharisees. So the Pharisees began to feel that they were more obedient to God's commands than other people were. And they felt they needed to watch everyone else to make sure they were obeying all the laws. The laws became so important to the Pharisees that they began to forget the real meaning, the spirit, of the Commandments, which was love for God and for others. Jesus, on the other hand, loved the true meaning of the Commandments. He taught people about God's love, and he proved this love by healing. If a Jewish law kept him from loving and healing, Jesus didn't obey it. This upset the Pharisees. It also bothered them that big crowds of people were following Jesus and not them.

He gave them a strong order. He said, "**Don't tell anyone** about this." Jesus probably knew that if these two men talked about their healings, some of the **scribes** and **Pharisees** might ask them questions they couldn't answer. Then the men might lose their faith in Jesus' healing power.

Because the men were so happy to be able to see again, it was hard to obey Jesus. They wanted to tell everyone they saw about their healing. And they did. Everywhere they went, they told how Jesus had healed them and how wonderful it was to see.

Man Healed of Dumbness

Matthew 9:32, 33

Jesus was in **Capernaum** on this day. And what a wonderful day full of healing it was! Earlier in the day he healed a woman who had been ill for many years. Then he brought a 12-year-old girl back to life. As he left her home, two blind men followed him into another house, and he healed them, too. ■

As the two men left, Jesus must have thanked God for this power to bless so many people. He knew that the happiest work of all is to heal and to teach others to heal. He once said, "The Father has not left me alone, for I always do what pleases him." ■

Just then, someone else who needed healing was brought to Jesus.

Capernaum: See page 16.

See the following stories:
☐ "Jairus' Daughter Brought Back to Life" on page 16.
☐ "Woman Healed of Illness" on page 25.
☐ "Two Men Healed of Blindness" on page 30.

See John 8:29.

Unclean Spirits, Evil Spirits, Demons, Devils, Unclean Devils: See page 8.

WHAT CAN YOU DO?

When you read and hear about how Jesus healed people and brought so much happiness, you may want to do that, too. You can! Just let yourself think and act the way Jesus did. First of all, Jesus loved God with all his heart, and he loved everyone else, too. He loved *God* by knowing He is everywhere and the only power. So, there isn't any room for bad thoughts or sickness or sadness. Jesus loved *everyone else* by seeing them as God's perfect, spiritual creation. This is the love that heals. When you're loving and wanting to be helpful as Jesus was, you'll find ways to heal wherever you are. God will be right there giving you just the right ideas you need.

This was a man who was dumb, which means he couldn't talk.

In those days people believed in invisible beings called **devils.** And they believed that a devil was keeping this man from being able to talk.

But Jesus knew that devils aren't real. He knew the truth about devils—that they are only bad thoughts that have no power because God and His good thoughts are the only power.

When the man was brought to Jesus to be healed, Jesus destroyed the devil, or bad thought, in an instant by knowing what was true. And when the bad thought was destroyed, the man could speak!

Just think what it meant to this man to be able to talk to others. He didn't have to be silent any more. He must have left that house shouting with joy!

When the crowd knew that Jesus healed this man, they were so amazed. Everyone was saying, "Healings like this have never been seen among the Jews!"

Heal the sick, cleanse the lepers, raise the dead, cast out devils.

Matthew 10:8

Jesus never doubted for a minute that God always loves and cares for His children. He wasn't afraid of what his eyes and ears told him—whether it was sickness, sin, or death. Instead, he knew the truth that God, who is Spirit, keeps everyone just the way He made them—in His image and likeness. He knew that since God's children reflect Him, they can't help but be good and healthy and harmonious all the time. Jesus expected his disciples to heal, too. He taught them how. And they healed people of sickness and sin and brought people back to life by knowing the truths Jesus knew. We're also disciples. We can do it, too!

Man Healed of Disability

John 5:1-15

Jerusalem: Jerusalem was the most important city in Bible times. It is in the center of the country up in the hills of Judea. David captured the city and made it the capital of his kingdom and the center of worship. Solomon built the first Temple here. (See **Temple** on page 41.) For centuries Jews traveled to Jerusalem to festivals held in the Temple. Jerusalem has had a long history of rulers and kings, war and peace, destruction and rebuilding. In Jesus' time the Romans ruled Jerusalem and the country of Palestine. The Bible tells of several times that Jesus was in Jerusalem.

Festivals: Jewish law provided for special religious celebrations each year called "feasts" or "festivals." Three were so important that the law required every Jewish male aged 13 and up to go to the Temple in Jerusalem to celebrate:
- Passover—Unleavened Bread
- Pentecost
- Feast of Tabernacles

Jesus also celebrated these feasts. (See **Temple** on page 41.)

Pool of Bethesda: This was a large pool, probably about the size of a football field. It had covered porches on four sides and a fifth porch down the center, dividing the pool into two.

Once Jesus went to **Jerusalem** during one of the **festivals.** While he was there, he walked to a place called the **Pool of Bethesda.**

The Bible says that "an angel went down at a certain season into the pool, and troubled the water: whosoever then first after the troubling of the water stepped in was made whole of whatsoever disease he had" (John 5:4). This verse was added to the story by someone other than the writer of the book of John. The reason for the addition may have been to explain the people's superstition about the movement of the water.

There are other explanations for the movement. It is possible that the source of the water was a spring and that the flow of the water wasn't steady. Any time the spring started up, it might have caused the water in the pool to bubble up. Another possibility is that the water flowed through underground pipes to this pool and other pools, and the flow of water to the various pools was not always a steady flow. It might have stopped and started from time to time, causing sudden movements in the water.

Many people who were sick, blind, or unable to walk were sitting or lying on the porches around the pool. Jesus probably knew that people who needed his help would be there.

People believed the water had special power to heal—but only when it was moving. █ And this happened only at certain times. The people believed that the first person to step into the water when it started bubbling would be healed. So everyone hoped to be the first one in.

But Jesus saw a man there who didn't look very hopeful.

Jesus may have asked the man if he wanted to be well in order to help him think about whether he *really* wanted to be healed. Perhaps this man wanted others to feel sorry for him and take care of him. Or, perhaps he was a beggar, and if he was healed, he would have to work to make a living. Or, maybe he had lost all hope that he could ever be healed. It's possible that Jesus asked this question in order to awaken faith in the man—to help him expect that he could be healed.

Sir/Lord: See page 30.

WHAT CAN YOU DO?

Have you ever felt that you needed a friend? You can know that God is your friend, who always loves you. You can look for good everywhere you are. Every time you see something good in your life—even the tiniest thing—that's just a peek at God's great love and friendship for you. The more carefully you watch, the more good you'll see and feel, because God's goodness is everywhere. And as you discover and feel God's love for *you*, you'll love others more and be a friend to *them*. There will be no room for loneliness!

This man had not been able to walk for 38 years. When Jesus saw the man, he didn't have to ask him if he had been there a long time. He knew! Jesus was always listening for God's thoughts, so he was able to know people's needs. He said to the man, "Do you want to be well?"

The man replied, "**Sir,** when the water moves, I don't have a friend to put me into the pool. While I'm trying to get to the water, someone else always steps in before me."

They that wait upon the Lord shall renew their strength; . . . they shall run, and not be weary; and they shall walk, and not faint.

Isaiah 40:31

Jesus helped this man trust God's goodness and power. He helped the man see that he could be free of the fear that he couldn't move like other people. When Jesus commanded him to get up, carry his bed, and walk, the man knew instantly that he was perfectly able to do this. He felt the energy of Spirit. God doesn't make us weak. He makes us perfect and strong. Jesus knew this and proved it. And we can, too.

Jesus told the man to do something that might have seemed impossible for someone who hadn't walked for a long time. He said firmly, "Rise, pick up your **bed**, and walk." He did not believe this man was weak and unable to walk. Instead, he knew that he was God's child—strong and active.

The man felt the power of Jesus' command, and he was changed immediately. Now he was able to walk away carrying the bed on his shoulder. How happy he must have been!

But some other people were not so happy about the healing.

John refers to the "Jews" here. These were probably the Jewish leaders or Pharisees (and possibly the scribes as well) who opposed Jesus. (See **Scribes, Pharisees** on page 32.)

Sabbath Laws: "Sabbath" in Hebrew means "rest." Genesis says that God "rested on the seventh day." The Jews call this day, which is Saturday, the "Sabbath." This is the day God knew that His creation was complete, and He blessed this day (Genesis 2:2, 3). The Fourth Commandment refers to this blessing: "Remember the sabbath day, to keep it holy" (Exodus 20:8). The Jews believed that the way to keep the Sabbath holy was to do no work. Their laws listed many things that should not be done on the Sabbath, including healing. But Jesus understood God's "Sabbath rest" in a deeper way. He knew that everything God created is good, and He keeps it that way. So Jesus "rested" as God did—satisfied in God's complete and perfect, spiritual creation. That kind of rest is active and good. It heals—every day. Jesus never stopped healing—no matter what day it was. He knew that doing good is the very best way to keep the Sabbath holy.

When the Jewish leaders ■ saw this man carrying his bed, they said to him, "This is the sabbath day. It is **against the law** for you to carry your bed today."

The man answered, "The man who healed me told me to pick up my bed and walk."

The Jews asked him, "Who was it that told you to take up your bed and walk?" But the man couldn't answer because he didn't know Jesus' name. He couldn't find Jesus to ask him because Jesus had disappeared into the crowd after the healing.

The man then went to the **Temple.** This was the most important place in the world for Jews to worship God.

When the man had been disabled and unable to move quickly, people believed he was "**unclean.**" Because of this, he had not been allowed to go to the Temple—that was the law. Now, how happy he was to be healed and to be able to worship God in the Temple.

Jesus went to the Temple, too. He found the man there and said to him, "Think about it! You have been healed. From now on, don't sin, because something worse may happen to you." Jesus was telling this man how important good thinking and acting were in order for him to stay well and happy.

The man left the Temple and told the Jewish leaders that Jesus was the man who had healed him. He loved sharing the good news!

Temple: The Temple in Jerusalem was the center of the Jews' religious worship. More than just a place of prayer and public worship, the Temple symbolized the presence of God. It was planned by King David almost 1,000 years before Jesus and was built by his son Solomon, when he became king. It was very large and beautiful and built by skilled workers using the finest wood, stone, silver, and gold. The Temple contained a room called the "Holy of Holies," where the ark was kept. The ark was a chest that contained Moses' Ten Commandments on stone tablets, as well as other articles. The ark had disappeared by Jesus' time.

The Temple was destroyed by an enemy in 586 B.C. and then rebuilt and finished in 515 B.C. King Herod the Great began to expand and rebuild the Temple in 20 B.C. It was finished in 64 A.D.

Jesus' parents took him to the Temple for a special ritual when he was a baby. And when he was 12 years old, he and his parents traveled from Nazareth to the Temple for a festival. Jesus stayed to listen to and question the teachers there. When Jesus grew up, he traveled to Jerusalem for festivals and sometimes taught in the Temple area. Once or twice Jesus made people leave this area when they did not treat it with respect.

Laws of Cleanness: See page 8.

Woman's Daughter Healed of Illness

Matthew 15:21-28

*Another account of this story is found in **Mark 7:24-30**.*

Jerusalem: See page 36.

Galilee: See page 6.

Disciples: See page 6.

Phoenicia: This was the region north of Palestine on the coast of the Mediterranean Sea. Tyre and Sidon were important cities in this region. The Phoenicians, or Canaanites, who lived there worshiped idols and had a long history as enemies of the Jews.

Gentiles: See page 7.

Mark says that Jesus "entered into an house, and would have no man know it" (Mark 7:24). The house Jesus entered was probably a Gentile house. If so, Jesus was not obeying a Jewish law of cleanness. (See **Laws of Cleanness** on page 8.)

Jesus taught and healed people from Phoenicia. He spoke of their faith and willingness to learn. (See Mark 3:8; Luke 6:17-19; Luke 10:13.)

Jesus had been in **Jerusalem,** where he healed a man who had been disabled for 38 years. When he returned home to **Galilee,** people brought him many who were sick, and he healed them, too.

One day Jesus left Galilee with his **disciples** and traveled to **Phoenicia.** Many **Gentiles** lived there. Probably most of them didn't believe in the one God. But many from this area had gone to Galilee to hear Jesus and be healed.

A woman there,  who knew about Jesus and his healings, followed him, begging for help. This woman was very brave to talk to Jesus. People thought **women weren't as important as men** and shouldn't talk to them in public. She called out to him, "Have mercy on me, O **Lord**, Son of David!" This name meant "**Messiah**," or "**Christ**," a name the Jews used for a special king or prophet they believed would come one day to help and heal them. By calling Jesus this, the woman may have been showing him that she had faith he could help her. Next, she cried, "My daughter has a **devil** in her that is making her very sick."

In those days everybody—Gentiles and Jews—believed invisible beings called devils could get inside people and make them sick and mixed up. But Jesus knew that the only power anywhere is God's power of good. Therefore, there are no such things as devils, and there is no evil power that can make people sick or confused. Jesus knew that the woman's daughter was loved by God and that nothing bad could ever touch her.

Matthew describes her as "a woman of Canaan" (Matt 15:22). Mark says she was "a Greek, a Syrophoenician by nation" (Mark 7:26). Matthew and Mark make it clear that her background, culture, language, and religion are very different from that of Jesus.

Jesus' Treatment of Women: See page 28.

Sir/Lord: See page 30.

Messiah/Christ: See page 5.

Unclean Spirits, Evil Spirits, Demons, Devils, Unclean Devils: See page 8.

In *Jesus' Healings,* see the following stories:
- "Centurion's Servant Healed of Paralysis," (*Part 1,* page 38).
- "Man Healed of Mental Illness (Gadara)," (*Part 2,* page 6).

Jesus said he was sent to "the lost sheep of the house of Israel" (Matthew 15:24). "House of Israel" meant "Jews." "The lost sheep" could refer to:

- The *Amhaarez.* These were the laborers and country people considered outcasts by most Pharisees and scribes (see **Scribes, Pharisees** on page 32) because they didn't observe all the Pharisees' ritual laws. Perhaps Jesus meant he came to help and heal these humble people. (In Palestine's history, the term *Amhaarez* was also used to refer to Jews who married Gentiles like the Canaanites.)
- All the Jewish nation. Prophets had told of a Messiah who would be like a shepherd to the Jews (Ezekiel 34:11, 23). Jesus may have meant he was sent first to the Jews who were expecting such a shepherd.

Jesus began his work in Palestine, teaching and healing his fellow Jews. While he spent most of his time there, he also went to Gentile areas such as Samaria, Decapolis, Caesarea Philippi, and Phoenicia. And Gentiles came to him from these areas to hear him and to be healed. Jesus loved those who were considered outcasts—women, sinners, publicans, Gentiles. He showed his appreciation for their faith, and he taught and healed them. Also, at the end of his ministry, Jesus told his disciples to go and "teach all nations" (Matthew 28:19).

Jesus didn't answer the woman right away. He may have been testing his disciples to see what they would do. Jesus had taught his disciples the importance of loving others. But his disciples weren't loving this woman. Instead, they begged him, "Send her away. She keeps following us and calling out." But Jesus didn't send the woman away. He always helped those in need—both Jews and Gentiles. ■

He said to the disciples, "I've been sent to the Jews who are like lost sheep." ■ Jesus might have been saying that his mission was to help those Jews who were meek and willing to follow him the way sheep listen to and follow their shepherd. Although this woman was a Gentile, she, too, was meek and ready to listen to Jesus' words.

She fell down at Jesus' feet and begged him, "Lord, help me!" Because Jesus was always listening to God, he already knew how much she loved her daughter and wanted her to be healed. He knew this woman had **faith** that he could heal her child. He knew she wouldn't give up.

Both Jesus and the woman knew his disciples thought Jesus shouldn't help her because she was a Gentile. So he said out loud what his disciples might have been thinking. He said, "It isn't right to take the children's bread and give it to young dogs." Here, the word "children" meant the Jews. "Bread" meant God's goodness, love, and healing power. And "young dogs" meant the Gentiles. Jews often called Gentiles "dogs" because they thought Gentiles were "**unclean,**" or impure—like dogs.

Jesus knew the woman would give a great answer to show the disciples that she deserved his help.

Healing by Faith: See page 20.

Laws of Cleanness: See page 8.

The Bible records only one other person whom Jesus praised for his great faith. This was the Roman centurion—who was also a Gentile. (See Matthew 8:10; Luke 7:9.) (See "Centurion's Servant Healed of Paralysis," *Jesus' Healings, Part 1,* page 38.)

There is neither Jew nor Greek, there is neither bond nor free, there is neither male nor female: for ye are all one in Christ Jesus.

Galatians 3:28

Jesus knew that God, Spirit, is the only creator. This means that everyone He has created is spiritual and good. It doesn't matter whether people are Jew or Greek, slave or free, male or female—God sees them as spiritual. Jesus always saw everyone this way, too. And he knew that each one is God's favorite child! Because of that, no matter who needed healing, Jesus was ready to help—to see God's healing power right at hand. Like Jesus, we can know that everyone is created and loved equally by God. As we follow Christ Jesus' example, we'll be willing to help anyone who needs healing. We'll also be helping to bring peace to the whole world.

And she did have a good answer. She said, "It's true, Lord, but the young dogs eat the crumbs that fall from their master's table." She understood that in God's family, there is enough love to heal everyone—the children and the young dogs! The Jews *and* the Gentiles!

Jesus certainly knew that, too. He knew that God created everything and everyone and that He cares for all, forever. God doesn't have favorites and give more good to some people than to others. He loves all equally. Jews and Gentiles. Men and women. Boys and girls.

Jesus answered the woman with such joy: "O woman! You have great faith!" ■ He could see how much she trusted in God's goodness.

And how wonderful it was for the disciples to see that this Gentile woman was indeed a person of great faith and deserved Jesus' help.

Then Jesus said what she wanted so much to hear.

Mark tells us that Jesus said, "For this saying go thy way; the devil is gone out of thy daughter" (Mark 7:29). Jesus was pleased by the woman's response. She not only had great faith but also was able to express herself in a delightful way, using the same ideas Jesus had used—children, young dogs, crumbs from the table.

Mark also tells us that the woman went to her house and "found the devil gone out, and her daughter laid upon the bed" (Mark 7:30). Her daughter was free of her illness and resting on her bed.

He told her, "What you have wanted has happened." And at that very moment, her daughter was completely well. ▧ Jesus had never believed the lie that she was sick. He knew the truth that God is all powerful and was always taking care of her. And this truth healed her, even when she was someplace else.

This woman knew her daughter had been healed. She had believed and trusted that there was a God who could heal. She had made the effort to find Jesus, the man who understood God's healing love better than anyone else. She had expected healing and had not given up. Trusting in God and expecting good always brings good.

What a happy day for the woman and her daughter! And what a good lesson for Jesus' disciples to learn— that God's love and healing power are always right at hand for everyone.

WHAT CAN YOU DO?

Sometimes when you need to be healed, you might get discouraged. Maybe you think you aren't good enough to be healed, or your problem is too hard, or you're far away from God. All these thoughts are lies. You don't have to believe them. The woman in this story didn't listen to any of these lies. She expected her daughter to be healed. And so did Jesus. He knew God loves every one of His children completely. He knew God's healing power is everywhere and all-powerful. God is right where you are and loves you more than you can even imagine. You can expect healing, too!

Man Healed of Deafness and Speech Problems

Mark 7:31-37

Phoenicia: See page 42.

Gentiles: See page 7.

Galilee: See page 6.

Jordan River: In the Bible the Jordan is an important river and is mentioned often. Elisha directed Naaman to wash in the Jordan to be healed of leprosy. John the Baptist preached by the Jordan and baptized Jesus there. The Jordan River flows from the mountains in the north into a lake called the Sea of Galilee, then on down through the Jordan Valley until it reaches the Dead Sea, the lowest spot on earth, 1,300 feet below sea level.

Decapolis: See page 7.

The Bible says they asked Jesus "to put his hand upon him" (Mark 7:32). (See **Laying on of Hands/Healing by Touch** on page 17.)

Jesus had been in **Phoenicia,** where he healed the daughter of a **Gentile** woman.

Instead of going back to his own country of **Galilee,** he crossed the **Jordan River** and traveled to **Decapolis.** Large crowds followed him. Most of the people there were Gentiles, and many had heard of Jesus.

When he arrived, people brought a man to him who couldn't hear and couldn't speak clearly. The people who brought him begged Jesus to **heal their friend.** ▪

Jesus took the man away from the crowd so that the two of them could be alone. Because the man couldn't hear, Jesus used a kind of sign language to help him understand that he would heal him. First, Jesus touched the man's ears to show him that he would be healed of deafness. Next, he touched the man's tongue to show him that he would be healed of his speech problems. ■

Then, Jesus looked up to the sky. This was another signal to help the man have better and higher thoughts—to look away from his problem and think about God as the healing power. When people looked up like Jesus did, it was a way of saying that they were listening to God. This man might have been a Gentile who believed in many different gods. But Jesus wanted him to have faith that there is only one God, who is good, all-powerful, and everywhere.

Here, the Bible says that Jesus "spit, and touched his tongue" (Mark 7:33). (See **Spit** below.)

Spit: In Jesus' time spit had at least two symbolic meanings:
■ *Healing*—People thought of spit as a remedy for small wounds. So spit became a symbol for healing. Perhaps Jesus used spit in a few of his healings to help people understand that he was going to heal them. Jesus knew that spit had no power to heal. And no one would have thought that touching parts of the face with spit could heal deafness, speech problems, or blindness. (See **Laying on of Hands/Healing by Touch** on page 17.)
■ *Disapproval*—Spitting also showed that something was worthless. When Jesus spit, he was rejecting any thought that the power to see, hear, or speak comes from people's eyes, ears, or tongues. Jesus knew that this power comes only from God.

Mark tells us that Jesus said, *"Ephphatha"* in Aramaic, the language he spoke (Mark 7:34). In Greek, the language of Decapolis, the word means "Be opened!"

WHAT CAN YOU DO?

Maybe someone you know is hard to talk to because he or she has a handicap. Jesus found ways to talk to the man in this story who couldn't hear or talk. Jesus used sign language to tell the man he would heal him. When you love others as Jesus loved, you can find just the right way to let them know you love them and want to help them. God wants you to love others and be their friend. If you turn to God as Jesus did, you'll find He is showing you lots of ways to love.

Next, Jesus breathed a deep sigh. This may have been a way for Jesus to show the man that he was listening to God and His messages of love and healing—and listening with all his might.

Then Jesus spoke to the man for the first time. He commanded, "Be opened!" ▧

Jesus expected the man to hear, understand, and obey this order. He knew that since God is Spirit and all powerful, His children are spiritual, perfect, and free. He knew that nothing could keep this man from being free. God made His children to hear and speak perfectly.

The word is very nigh unto thee, in thy mouth, and in thy heart, that thou mayest do it.

Deuteronomy 30:14

God's word—His messages of love and truth—are as close as the words in our mouths or the thoughts in our hearts. As we listen to God and are grateful for His great goodness, we'll hear just what will bless us and others. When Jesus met people who couldn't hear or speak, he didn't believe this was true about them. He knew all of God's children reflect the perfect hearing and perfect speech of their Creator. Jesus' listening to God's messages and knowing what was true brought healing. As we listen to these messages, we, too, will hear God telling us what to know and what to say, and this will bring healing to others as well as to ourselves.

"Don't tell anyone. . . .":
See page 24.

The instant that Jesus said, "Be opened," it happened! Not only did the man hear, but he began to speak clearly, too.

Then, Jesus ordered the people **not to tell anyone** about the healing.

But the man who was healed and the people who saw it happen wanted to tell others about this wonderful healing. Even though Jesus told them many times to be quiet, the man and his friends just kept telling more people about it.

Everyone who heard the story was amazed. They all said, "Jesus can do everything and do it perfectly. He can make people hear *and* speak."

Man Healed of Blindness

Mark 8:22-26

Bethsaida: This city is located in a region called Gaulanitis. (See **Gaulanitis** below.) Bethsaida was the hometown of Peter, Andrew, and Philip and possibly more of the disciples.

Gaulanitis: This region was on the east side of the Sea of Galilee.

Bethsaida was one of the three cities where most of Jesus' healings took place. But Jesus rebuked the people there for not changing their thinking after seeing his mighty healing works (Matthew 11:20, 21).

Mark says they "besought him to touch him" (Mark 8:22). See **Laying on of Hands/Healing by Touch,** page 17.

See the following stories in which Jesus prepared a quiet, peaceful place for healing:
☐ "Jairus' Daughter Brought Back to Life" on page 16.
☐ "Two Men Healed of Blindness" on page 30.
☐ "Man Healed of Deafness and Speech Problems" on page 48.

After healing a man of deafness and speech problems, Jesus traveled to **Bethsaida.** He was well-known in Bethsaida because he had healed many people there. ■ But the people in the town didn't really listen to Jesus or follow him.

Some people in the town brought a blind man to Jesus and begged him to heal him. ■ The first thing Jesus did was to take the blind man by the hand and lead him out of town. Jesus must have wanted to be alone with the man and away from the people of Bethsaida who had so little faith in his healing power. ■

When they were out of town, Jesus lovingly showed the blind man that he would be healed. First, he touched the man's eyes. He was helping the man expect healing. Then, he put his hands on him to comfort him.

Next, Jesus asked him if he saw anything. The man looked and said, "I can see people, but they look like trees walking around." The man could see a little, but he wasn't completely healed.

Jesus knew that God's healing power didn't stop when someone got a little better. So Jesus kept praying—knowing the truth about the man—that it was natural for a child of God to have perfect sight. Then, he touched the man's eyes again to let him know he was still with him and praying and to encourage him to keep expecting good.

The man opened his eyes and looked, and this time he was able to see clearly. What a great feeling it must have been to be able to see!

And how grateful he must have been to Jesus for not giving up!

Here, the Bible says that Jesus "spit on his eyes, and put his hands upon him" (Mark 8:23). (See **Spit** on page 49 and **Laying on of Hands/Healing by Touch** on page 17.)

WHAT CAN YOU DO?

Sometimes when you pray, you may feel your prayers aren't answered right away. Or you may get only part of the answer to your prayers. You may even lose hope and think your prayers have failed. But prayer is a lot like working on a project at school. You need to keep working on it until it's finished.

Jesus showed the blind man that he should keep expecting to be healed. You can do that, too. Keep praying. Keep listening to God's angel messages. God loves you and has only good for you. God's guidance and healing power never stop. When you keep trusting God's love and listening for His messages, you will learn wonderful new things about God and about yourself. And you will find complete healing.

"Don't tell anyone....":
See page 24.

*Be ye stedfast,
unmoveable, always
abounding in the work
of the Lord.*

I Corinthians 15:58

Jesus knew that God naturally gives His children perfect sight. When this man's eyesight didn't seem completely clear, Jesus didn't give up. And he wouldn't let the man give up either. Jesus always turned to God in prayer for healing. And he knew God doesn't answer prayer halfway. No matter what the man said about his eyes, Jesus stayed firm, knowing that God always keeps his children perfect in every way.

Jesus knew that if he kept his thought filled with what was really true about this man, they would both see the results of his prayer — and they did. Each of us has the same ability to be steadfast. We can hold on to the truth, just as Jesus did, no matter what. And we'll find healing, too.

Jesus then told the man, "Go straight home. Don't go into the town. And **don't tell anyone** from town about your healing."

Perhaps Jesus felt that the people of Bethsaida had so little faith in the power of God to heal that they might question the man and argue with him. Jesus must have wanted this man to have a quiet time by himself to think about his healing and be grateful for his new faith in God's power.

Man's Son Healed of Epilepsy

Matthew 17:14-21

*Other accounts of this story are found in **Mark 9:17-29** and **Luke 9:37-42**.*

Bethsaida: See page 52.

Disciples: See page 6.

This could have been Mount Hermon, the highest mountain in Palestine. Its snow-covered peaks can be seen for many miles.

Luke says this was the man's only child (Luke 9:38).

Sir/Lord: See page 30.

Matthew says the boy was "lunatick" (Matthew 17:15). Mark says he had a "a dumb spirit" (Mark 9:17). Today, this sickness is called "epilepsy."

Unclean Spirits, Evil Spirits, Demons, Unclean Devils, Devils: See page 8.

After healing a blind man near **Bethsaida**, Jesus led his **disciples** to a mountain. ■ While nine of the disciples waited at the bottom of the mountain, Jesus took the other three up with him to teach them important lessons.

When Jesus and the three disciples came down, a man who was very worried about his son ■ saw Jesus and went to him. This man kneeled at Jesus' feet and begged him for help. He said, "**Lord,** have mercy on my son! He has a terrible sickness ■ because a **devil** is controlling him. Often, he is wild and falls into the fire or the water and hurts himself." People believed that devils were invisible beings that could get inside people and make them sick or wild. But Jesus knew that devils were only wrong thoughts, or lies. He knew that God is the only power and destroys these lies.

The father said, "I brought him to your disciples, but they couldn't heal him."

Healing by Faith: See page 20.

Commit thy way unto the Lord; trust also in him; and he shall bring it to pass.

Ps 37:5

When we commit our life to God, that means we are taking a stand for what is right and good. We're trusting that God is all-powerful and the only presence—no matter what we see with our eyes or what people tell us. We're knowing without a doubt that God made us in His image and that He always guides and guards us. This faith in God's great power and goodness destroys sickness now just as it did in Jesus' time.

The father, the disciples, and the crowd all waited to hear what Jesus would say. He spoke strong words, which were probably meant for the disciples: "How unbelieving you are! You've turned away from what you learned—that God is the only power! How long will I have to be with you before you understand? How many times do you have to hear this?"

The disciples had heard Jesus talk about God's power so many times. They had seen so many wonderful healings. Jesus had been teaching and proving that there is nothing impossible to God. He wanted the disciples—and everyone else—to understand how natural it was to heal when one simply had complete faith in God.

Jesus then said to the father, "Bring your son to me."

Jesus' faith was strong and constant. He knew that God is good and gives His children only good health. This boy's sickness wasn't good and God wouldn't allow it. It just had no power.

When the boy was brought to him,  Jesus spoke firmly to the devil, or wrong thought. And the boy was healed—right then!

How thankful and happy the boy's father must have been to see his son completely well!

Mark says that Jesus asked the father how long the boy had been sick. The father told him that he had been that way since he was a child. Jesus also told the father that all things were possible if he would believe. Perhaps Jesus was helping the father see that no matter how long the child had been sick, faith in God could heal him. Then the father, with tears in his eyes, cried out that he *did* believe. He asked Jesus to help him with the doubts he still had. Next, Jesus saw a large crowd moving toward them. Immediately, he called the devil, or evil spirit, by name—"dumb and deaf spirit"—and destroyed it. The boy screamed and fell down. People thought he was dead, but Jesus took his hand and helped him up (Mark 9:21, 23-27).

Casting Out Devils: See page 9.

Here, Matthew and Mark say that Jesus continued his discussion with his disciples (Matthew 17:19, 21; Mark 9:28, 29). He told them that cases like this could be healed only by "prayer and fasting." "Fasting" can mean "not eating." During Jesus' time, Jews fasted at various times—at someone's death, before a war, on special occasions such as the Day of Atonement. But Jesus didn't fast like this, and he didn't require his disciples to do this either. When he told his disciples that they could heal this boy only by prayer and fasting, he meant "fasting" in a different way. He meant they should not take into their thought the fearful things they saw with their eyes. Instead, they needed to pray—to let their thought be filled with God's power and love for this boy.

WHAT CAN YOU DO?

When someone you know is sick, you may be tempted to be afraid or to believe that God can't help that person. Jesus told his disciples to have faith—to trust in God's all-power. He knew that with even just a little faith a person can do what seems impossible. He told his disciples that if they had faith even as small as a mustard seed (which is very little), it would be enough to do great things. Faith in God means keeping your thought only on His wonderful love and great power.

With this faith, you can see that sickness is not a big impossible thing to heal. Faith can move mountains!

Afterwards, the disciples stepped away from the crowd and spoke to Jesus. They asked him why they hadn't been able to heal the boy. Jesus said to them, "Because you didn't have faith. You didn't trust that God is the only power."

Then he told them something to help them understand. He wanted them to see that even a *little* faith was very powerful. He said, "If you have faith even as small as a mustard seed, you'll be able to do great things. You can tell a mountain to move to another place and it will happen. Nothing will be impossible to you." When Jesus told them they could move mountains, it was like saying they could heal anything if they had faith.

How grateful the disciples must have been to have a better understanding of the power of faith in God! It was another great lesson from their teacher that would help them become better healers.

Bibliography

GENERAL

Deen, Edith. *All of The Women of The Bible*. San Francisco: Harper & Row, 1955.

Eddy, Mary Baker. *Prose Works other than Science and Health with Key to the Scriptures*. Boston: The First Church of Christ, Scientist, 1953.

Eddy, Mary Baker. *Science and Health with Key to the Scriptures*. Boston: The First Church of Christ, Scientist, 1934.

Harris, Stephen L. *The New Testament, A Student's Introduction*. Mountain View: Mayfield, 1995.

Kee, Howard Clark, Young, Franklin W., Froehlich, Karlfried. *Understanding The New Testament*. Englewood Cliffs: Prentice-Hall, 1965.

Mann, Thomas W. *The Book of the Torah*. Atlanta: John Knox, 1988.

Robinson, Russell D. *Teaching the Scriptures*. Milwaukee: Bible Study, 1993.

Sergio, Lisa. *Jesus and Woman*. McLean: EPM, 1975.

Trench, Richard C. *Notes on the Miracles of Our Lord*. Grand Rapids: Baker, 1949.

Trueblood, Elton. *The Humor of Christ*. San Francisco: Harper & Row, 1964.

BIBLES

Amplified Bible. Grand Rapids: Zondervan, 1965.

Gaus, Andy. *The Unvarnished New Testament*. Grand Rapids: Phanes, 1991.

Good News Bible, The Bible in Today's English Version. Nashville: Thomas Nelson, 1976.

The Living Bible. Wheaton: Tyndale, 1976.

Hastings, Selina. *The Children's Illustrated Bible*. New York: DK, 1994.

The Holy Bible. Authorized King James Version. New York: Oxford University.

The Illustrated Family Bible. Edited by Claude-Bernard Costecalde. New York: DK, 1997.

New Jerusalem Bible. New York: Doubleday, 1990.

New Living Translation. Wheaton: Tyndale, 1996.

New International Version. Wheaton: Tyndale, 1984.

Peterson, Eugene H. *The Message*. Colorado Springs: Navpress, 1995.

Phillips, J.B. *The New Testament in Modern English*. New York: Macmillan, 1972.

DICTIONARIES AND CONCORDANCES

The Anchor Bible Dictionary. Edited by David Noel Freedman. New York: Doubleday, 1992.

Dictionary of Judaism in the Biblical Period. Edited by Jacob Neusner. Peabody: Hendrickson, 1966.

Dictionary of the Bible. Edited by James Hastings. New York: Charles Scribner's Sons, 1963.

HarperCollins Bible Dictionary. San Francisco: Harper. 1996.

Illustrated Dictionary of Bible Life and Times. Pleasantville: Reader's Digest, 1997.

International Standard Bible Encyclopedia Electronic Edition STEP Files. Parsons Technology, 1998.

The Interpreter's Dictionary of the Bible. Edited by George Arthur Buttrick. Nashville: Abingdon, 1962.

Quick Verse for Windows Version 5.0c. Cedar Rapids: Parsons Technology, 1992-1998:

    Holman Bible Dictionary. Edited by Trent C. Butler.

    International Standard Bible Encyclopedia. Edited by James Orr, 1998.

Strong, James. *The Exhaustive Concordance of The Bible.* Nashville: Abingdon, 1980.

Thayer, Joseph H. *Thayer's Greek-English Lexicon of the New Testament.* Grand Rapids: Baker, 1977.

COMMENTARIES

Barclay, William. *The Daily Study Bible.* Philadelphia: Westminster, 1975.

A Commentary on The Holy Bible. Edited by Rev. J.R. Dummelow. New York: Macmillan, 1939.

The Expositor's Bible Commentary. Edited by Frank E. Gaebelein. Grand Rapids: Zondervan, 1984.

Harper's Bible Commentary. Edited by James L. Mays. San Francisco: Harper & Row, 1988.

The Interpreter's Bible. Nashville: Abingdon, 1982.

The Interpreter's One-Volume Commentary on the Bible. Edited by Charles M. Laymon. Nashville: Abingdon, 1971.

JFB Commentary on The Whole Bible. Edited by Robert Jamieson, A.E. Fausset, David Brown. Grand Rapids: Zondervan, 1961.

Henry, Matthew. *Matthew Henry's Commentary on the Whole Bible.* New York: Fleming H. Revell.

The New Interpreter's Bible. Edited by Leander E. Keck. Nashville: Abingdon, 1995.

Stern, David S. *Jewish New Testament Commentary.* Clarksville, MD: Jewish New Testament Publications, Inc. 1995.

The Tyndale New Testament Commentaries. Edited by Canon Leon Morris. Grand Rapids: William B. Eerdmans, 1985.

The Wycliffe Bible Commentary. Edited by Everett G. Harrison. Nashville: Southwestern, 1962.

ATLASES

Atlas of the Bible Lands. Edited by Harry Thomas Frank. Maplewood, NJ: Hammond, 1990.

Oxford Bible Atlas. Edited by Herbert G. May. London: Oxford University, 1976.

DAILY LIFE IN BIBLE TIMES

Connolly, Peter. *Living in the Time of Jesus of Nazareth.* Israel: Steimatzky, 1983.

Derrett, J. Duncan M. *Jesus's Audience.* New York: Seabury, 1973.

Gower, Ralph. *The New Manners and Customs of Bible Times.* Chicago: Moody Press, 1987.

Great People of the Bible and How They Lived. Pleasantville: Reader's Digest, 1974.

Harper's Encyclopedia of Bible Life. Madeleine S. and J. Lane Miller. Edison: Castle, 1978.

Jesus and His Times. Edited by Kaari Ward. Pleasantville: Reader's Digest, 1987.

Thompson, J.A. *Handbook of Life in Bible Times.* Madison: Inter-Varsity, 1986.

Index to "What Can YOU Do?" Sidebars

Below are listed the "concerns" addressed in sidebars.

Index to Bible Verses

With this index, you will be able to find Bible verses in the stories and sidebars. In some cases, the Bible verses are paraphrased, rather than quoted or referenced. Bible books, chapters, and verses below are in the left column and in bold type. Page numbers are to the right of the verses. Page numbers in bold type indicate this verse is the subject of a sidebar.

General Index